SUGAR SKULLS

Coloring Pages for Halloween & the Day of the Dead
(*El Día de los Muertos*)

Hands-On Art History

Published in the United States by Hands-On Art History. For bulk sales, email blueivypress@gmail.com.

Sugar Skulls
Coloring Pages for Halloween & the Day of the Dead
Hands-On Art History —1st ed.
ISBN 978-1-948344-20-3

FREE COLORING PAGES

Sign up to get free art-related coloring pages
delivered to your inbox each month!

www.HandsOnArtHistory.com

Join the Coloring Club!

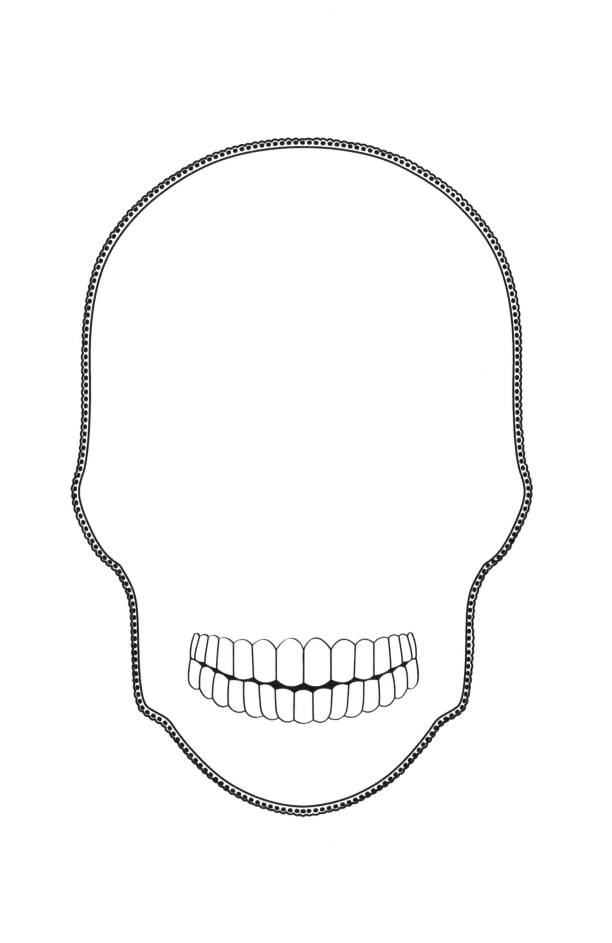

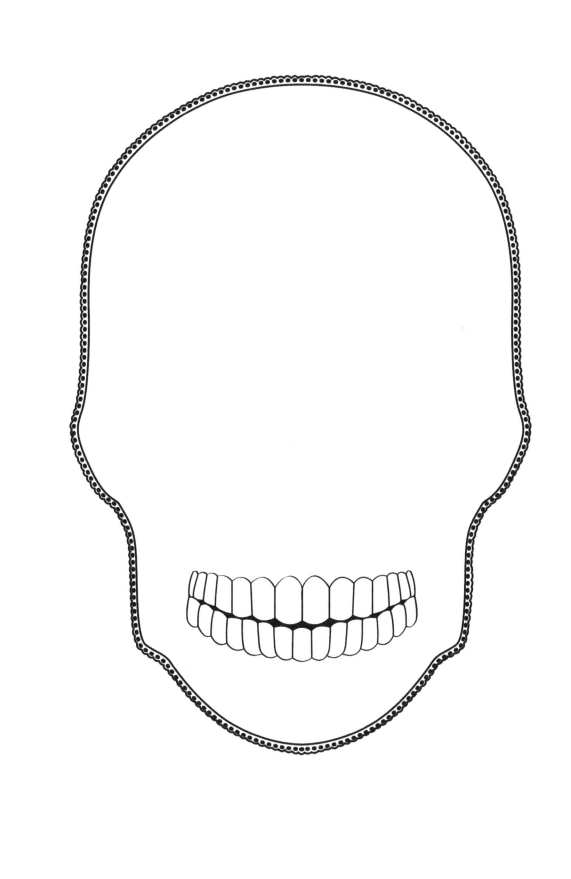

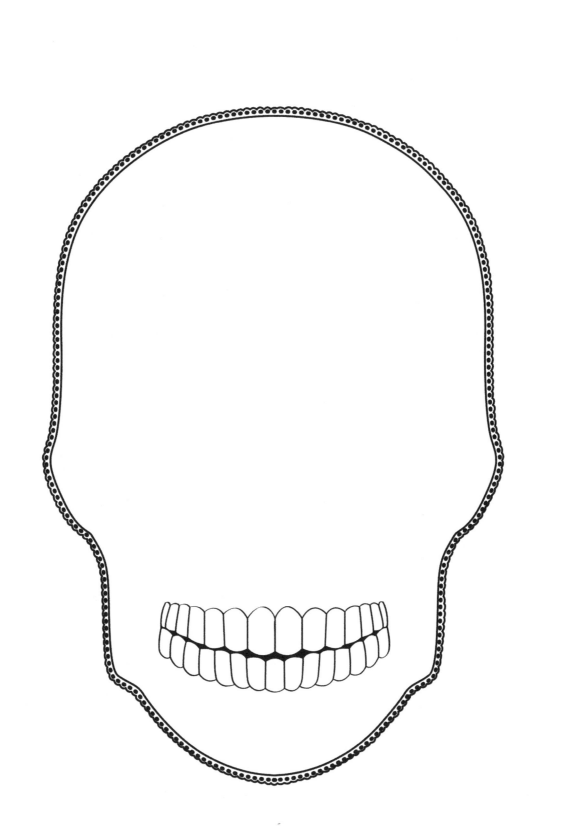

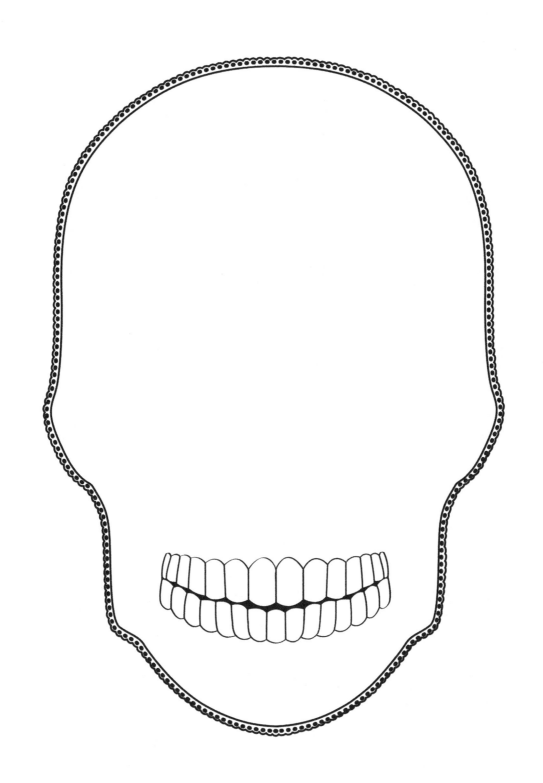

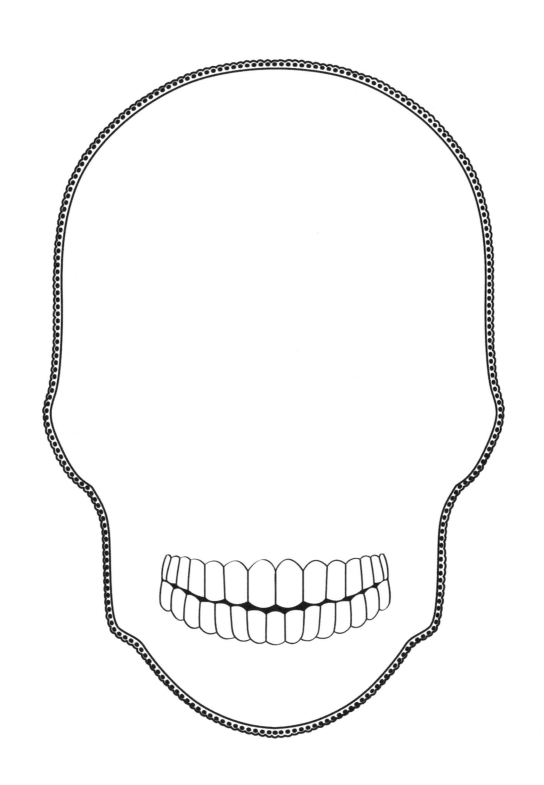

Made in the USA
Las Vegas, NV
10 October 2021